The Dream of Falling

poems by

Cynthia McCain

Finishing Line Press
Georgetown, Kentucky

The Dream of Falling

Copyright © 2020 by Cynthia McCain
ISBN 978-1-64662-198-9 First Edition
All rights reserved under International and Pan-American Copyright Conventions. No part of this book may be reproduced in any manner whatsoever without written permission from the publisher, except in the case of brief quotations embodied in critical articles and reviews.

ACKNOWLEDGMENTS

This book is for my family.

Publisher: Leah Maines
Editor: Christen Kincaid
Cover Art: Cynthia McCain
Author Photo: Karl Maasdam
Cover Design: Elizabeth Maines McCleavy

Printed in the USA on acid-free paper.
Order online: www.finishinglinepress.com
also available on amazon.com

Author inquiries and mail orders:
Finishing Line Press
P. O. Box 1626
Georgetown, Kentucky 40324
U. S. A.

Table of Contents

Cultural Immersion ... 1
Chestnut-backed Chickadee ... 3
Thimbleberry ... 4
Late ... 5
Las Viudas ... 6
Soul Mates ... 7
About Her Skin ... 8
Cold Rain ... 9
LaBarge Meadow ... 10
Herons 1 ... 11
Herons 2 ... 11
August Walk ... 12
This Morning ... 13
Book Club ... 14
Mutant Hippos of the Limpopo ... 15
River Traffic ... 16
More Hippos ... 17
I've Been Thinking a Lot about Hippos ... 18
Untitled ... 19
Gate ... 20
Tomato ... 21
X-rated ... 22
Hardware ... 23
A Recording of the Last Moments ... 24
The Color of Ice ... 25
The Dream of Falling ... 26
In Praise of Solitary Walks ... 27
Broken Boat ... 28
Widow's Waltz ... 29
Lullaby for the Inner Critic ... 30
Finding the True Root of the Moon ... 31
Last Dark/First Light ... 32
Flamenco Workshop ... 33
Can Memory Sleep ... 35

Cultural Immersion

I.

It's not that I feel guilty.

I took off the slipcovers.
I cried in public.
I didn't want to sing at the party.
I did not give enough gifts.
I asked for my first name.

when she took my arm, crossing the street
when they pushed me, squeezing into the bus
when I missed the train, the crowd swarming like bees
bones on the restaurant table

II.

It was a coal city in Heilongjiang.
There was a two-story brick tower
not far from the foreigners' hostel
that may have been for power,
hot water,
a boiler, maybe.
I don't know.
I grew up in California.
We bought electricity pre-wrapped in plastic at Safeway.

There were white cotton slipcovers on the flesh-colored chairs
in the foreigners' hostel.
One more layer between me and the world.
I uncovered the desk chair
in the name of freedom
and claustrophobia.
By the end of the year the chair was gray.

III.

We are cultured
like pearls.

Chestnut-backed Chickadee

Because I can name them, I think that I know them
but I don't know where they'll sleep tonight.
Is the leader of their flock a male, strong and dour?
Or a female, certain and impatient?
Are chickadees ever alone?
In winter they join with nuthatches, creepers, kinglets—
a tiny festival touring the trees together.
Why?

Because I can hear them, I feel at home here
but I don't know what the familiar sounds mean.
There's that call and a gurgle. This is mine. This is ours.
If a jay comes too close, a cloud of birdlets cage it in a cacophony
    of dees.

Now this I have never seen, but it's in the books:
in spring, in a cavity hollowed into a rotten tree,
the chickadees tuck a home-woven fur comforter
over their handful of nut-sized eggs.

How much of the natural history we learn is true,
and how much do we take on faith?
What is there to hear that no one knows to listen for?

Thimbleberry

I have never picked a thimbleberry,
though my mother gave me one of her thimbles
and my daughter borrowed it.

What I know of thimbleberries:
the leaves and the flower.
Thimbleberry leaves,
large, maple-shaped, flannel.
Thimbleberry flowers,
every inch a rose, but plain white, single, simple.

I don't understand what thimbleberries need
beyond sun, a chance to see the sky, enough water to share.

Thimbleberries along the trail, along the road,
in the butterfly meadow at Ollalie Mountain.
I have carried thimbleberry leaves in my pocket, walking along
as if I held my mother's hand.

Late

The phone does not bring good news
at three o'clock in the morning.
We wrap up together, we
who had been sleeping near the borders of the bed.

Four o'clock isn't good for much. It's too late or too early.
Even worry is worn out by four o'clock.
We fall asleep touching.

Las Viudas
> *(the widows)*

Tall, rough-skinned, high crowned,
dressed in moss and pale lichen.
Some spruce are stately, sober, joined solidly to the earth.
Others stand above a gap bridged by roots not meant to bear that weight.
They grew, seedling and slender sapling, on logs that promised
to lift them above the shadowed forest floor.
Many grew on logs too big, or too soon decayed, and will fall early.
Some have built their own base, grown great and old.
They stand straight in hard-won symmetry.
These old ones are still marked by trusting to forever;
there will always be some space beneath their roots.

I know a woman widowed in middle age.
She has soft arms, a rounded back, brown eyes like pansies.
In fifty years, no one has kissed her, nestled into her honey neck.

Dancing. They met, dancing.
She made do.
Her knees are worn out, she says. She doesn't walk anymore.

On the coast, storm winds roll through the tall spruce.
When some fall, their roots wrenched out of the dark earth,
the slopes unravel for years after.

Soul Mates

There are, what, seven billion people in the world now?
If your soul mate,
that one in a million,
lock to your key,
perfect fit,
hasn't found you yet,
do not, sweetheart, do not give up.
Seven billion is seven thousand million.
Therefore, my sweet, there are not one,
not two,
not two hundred,
but seven thousand of them out there.
Seven thousand hearts that beat as one.
In fact, a dime a dozen,
a veritable Valentines Day Massacre.
And so, at six degrees of separation,
you certainly know someone
who knows someone
who knows
and yet you don't
no one ever
no one
I know
and maybe that's for the best.

About Her Skin

The way you can see through it,
what you can see through her skin:
the blood under her skin, the color of the blood,
that purple red brown star of blood on the back of her hand,
the way the veins show through,
as though only the poverty blood,
lightened of its load of oxygen,
belongs in her now.

The way the wrist looks ornamental, not for everyday use.
The way my skin looks beside hers, her hand on my right hand.
Two different organs: hers a window, mine a wall.
Her body is sublimating.
Where did her skin go?

I take a picture like an X-ray, like the MRI,
like those images that have brought her here,
transparent and transient.

Cold Rain

Annunciation of queencup beadlily,
two single leaves
lone silent angel.

LaBarge Meadow

Twice so far at dusk
we've heard the clack of sandhill cranes
then seen them
wheeling back from the willow-filled valley
over the flower-curved hill across from the cabin.

The wind blows up the pass
while we wait for sunset.

People, horses, and cattle by the thousands once walked the Lander Cutoff,
heading west on the Oregon Trail.
They rested in these meadows and moved on.

If the pair of cranes come back this evening
they may be nesting along the creek
staying for the short summer along the Divide.

Herons 1

Herons land in trees
like trapeze artists
like tightrope walkers.

Herons 2

Herons come back home
to nests in bare cottonwoods
then draw the curtains.

August Walk

The meadow drapes over the knees of the hill
loose knit in beige and bone.
Heavy headed grasses almost hide
pink evening primroses
blooming during these curling days.
Hot tarweed breathes out musky August.
We walk up the steep trail at the speed of bees
visiting the last of summer.

This Morning

The children's bedrooms become
rooms of one's own
and also
on hollow occasion
private places for retreat
when the old single hallowed argument
drives us into our separateness.

Nothing is as full of symbols
as an empty bed.
Phyllis Diller, I read this in the paper, said
Don't go to sleep mad. Stay up and fight.
We're not alone.

This morning, I smooth down the quilt
where my husband washed up, but not for the whole long night.
In the summer sun, in Sunday's geometrical niceness
and rather friendly quiet,
I want to lie down.

I can hear the dog snoring under the bed.
She lives there in her safe den.
It's her retreat from life's alarms.
So perhaps this has become the dog's room
we only enter in our many moods
to borrow her canine dreams
of the perfect pack
the chase and eating
and one's own place and bed and sleep.

Book Club

Ladies at book club
careful not to say
what no one wants to hear.
Ladies at book club
startled to find out
how very different we are.
Ladies at book club
having opinions
all woven together
like making a basket.
We earn badges
in gentility, cancer, and eldercare.
We earn badges in association.

Mutant Hippos of the Limpopo

One hippopotamus.
Round, brown, nubbly,
bobbing basketball body.
Mouth wide, wider, no really, wider than that,
two marshmallow teeth between fluted tusks,
baby bear ears, peeping up on top.

Two hippopotami.
Backs, necks, breaking the surface.
Territorial, nocturnal,
exuding blood sweat. Blood sweat.
Swimming in the rivers.

Three hippopotami.
Four.

Many hippopotami,
all in the river,
in the Limpopo,
a flotilla
in the waters of Africa,
eyes on the top of the water.

One hippopotamus
yawning.

River Traffic

In the Magdalena River of Columbia
float the hippos of the Medellin cartel.

More Hippos

Another thing about hippos
is the hair around their ears sticking up out of the water,
bristles a grandfather could be proud of.

And the way they bounce like over-inflated elephants,
beach toys with mouths,
forty acres of tongue,
tusks that could hold up a parking garage.

They secrete their own sunscreen—
people used to call it blood sweat.

Put it on my list of things I won't be when I grow up:
astronaut
Antarctic explorer
biochemist studying mammalian skin secretions
underwater photographer filming elephants and hippos
flying
in the slow warm waters of other continents.

I've Been Thinking a Lot about Hippos

And clouds. It's been a great year for clouds. Maybe because I've been driving by myself in the country. Hills and valleys and fields wave and point and talk about them as they change and change. Problems, clouds. Two masses/necessities collide/slide past on curved brassy spheres, one warm, one cool, one dry, one weeping.

Hippos are discrete. See them from below. See the hippos swim, from the bed of the Limpopo, from the silty floor of the Magdalena. Cirrus hippos, cumulo-nimbus hippos. Hippos obscure the peaks. Massed hippos flying below the ridges, obscuring the peaks. Parades of pods of hippos interpreted by the weather-wise.

Think of rising into the cloud layers in a complex sky at the end of the day. Gold fans of late light beneath, over the hills and valleys that I drive. A last field illuminated.

Leave hippos alone. Reach out for clouds and hold on to time.

Untitled

I have a tree inside of me
the air is in eclipse
I wake up to memories in ice
my mother apologizes

nowhere is the tree minus the people
I can put the two together
though I am carefully not looking
I think there's more than one

with a tree inside of me
there are no end days, no subtraction
all colors frozen into eyes

Gate

The cat comes over to collect the toll
for crossing this bridge.
She takes the gate with her.

Tomato

The window painted shut
the glass gone
I put the empty frame in my garden
and walk past
the smell of ripening tomatoes

X-rated

My daughter texts
she needs some things she left behind in her dresser when she left for school.
She needs her sports bra
and some undies and posters for her wall.

I take the list to her empty room.
Sports bra—check.
One of mine she needed in a rush a couple of years ago
already.
Undies.
I pull out these butterflies
these posies
these secrets that Victoria whispered into
a flicking ear.
Striped sailors
polka dots
gold lame
leopard spots
black lace
cotton, nylon, a thong.
I never gave her those.
All I ever gave her was the second X.

So I seal them up in a left-over
bubble mailer
and put her east coast address in two places
just to make sure she gets what she needs.
But she should buy new posters.
She's outgrown these.

Hardware

The other day, a man said going to his family for love was like asking for bread in a hardware store.

In Corvallis, we have Robnett's Hardware, family owned since 1893 or thereabouts. Same building. Wood floors that have survived caulk boots and high heels.

You can go to Robnett's, and buy a single washer, a nut, or a cotter pin. They'll cut you a key. Tell you which switch you need. They look tired and there have been rumors of a chain but still they are my favorite store in town.

O, Robnett's.

Pack me a lunch.
Make it with bread
that you bought at Robnett's.
A peanut butter and screwdriver sandwich.
Pack it in a tool box.

A Recording of the Last Moments

the cry of a bird, cut off

the rocket,
deprived bird in winter plumage,
drops from the moonlit summer sky

a trail of hazard
the tiny cues

for the last acceleration
detached and falling

breast feathers
scattered
here and there

The Color of Ice

In the Arctic, in the farthest north Arctic,
where latitude and longitude converge,
the land is made of water.
The rocks and ridges and shadows are water.

The world is warming,
pushing polar bears off the polar ice
into towns and back porches and alleys,
where too much is soft.
.

Once the bears were the color of earth,
then the color of ice.
Soon they will be the color of air.

The Dream of Falling

There was a flower
and just for a moment
the flower was
only part
of a plant
a device for pollination,
bare of the exact glamor of beauty,
exposed to the adequate light of desolation.

In Praise of Solitary Walks

Crow tracks mark the damp sand as the tide ebbs. The trail ends at a dead starfish, where the narrow prints are deepest, each claw clear. That's where the crow went from sand to air. When the beach dries, the wind smooths out the one-way trail.

One winter morning, at the south end of Odell Lake, there were marks of a bird hunting near the shore. It had landed hard, then sliced long blue parallel shadows into the snow with cold wings. By afternoon, the sun erased the tracks.
It could have been an osprey.
It could have been an eagle.

A surf scoter dives in the woven waters between the waves at the beach off Newport. It leaves no evidence, no burrow in the roughened ocean, for those too late to see.

Broken Boat

Single handed__
I miss the quick, fluid, facile,
       and find the slow, persistent, stoic
I want to be deft;
       instead I am patient.

When I heal, I must learn
not to interrupt the slower side.

There is sweetness in taking care.

Give me a rowboat
for crossing the water
and I will row, and take my time.

Widow's Waltz

I see her in a cotton dress made of a tiny flower print, a dress with a skirt that flares just below her knees

and I see her turning and turning and the skirt spinning out like a paint wheel, like a dandelion blowing, like a sparkler twirling

and I hear her kissing the words and winding her mother around her fingers like a curl and tucking her daughter around her neck, catching her like a scarf as she circles and circles in a private waltz, scarf fluttering, flashing colors, flashing glints of gold and pain

and I see her with him on her shoulders and a lift and he rises from his wheel chair and alights en pointe and she swoons into his arms for the spotlight, she in a flowered skirt; he sinks to one knee, with her, eyes closed, her hands hanging to the stage, words in a pool, bright except where their shadows fall

Lullaby for the Inner Critic

you watch me
watch over me
don't
worry about me
stop
let me
see
your fierceness
your fear
always on duty
always here
let's stand in the open field
nothing is falling on us
no one is watching us
no one is coming towards us
relax in my arms
let your mouth
go
soft

Finding the True Root of the Moon

Old clear-cut
oak skeletons horizontal on the hill.
Walking the logging road
trailing the dog's slow rush
we pass through juncos
like passing through rain.

Last Dark/First Light

Night drains down into the valley.
The tired moon slowly searches for lost stars that slid down from the height.
The planets have gone.

At first light the horizon, a dream of the hills.
Distance develops in lines of fir.

Above the cold river, geese fly through the gallery of cottonwoods.
The shout of the vee, far off and unfollowed,
leaves no shadows,
leaves silence.

There is a rest between fall and springtime
that passes for winter where we live.
Hazel flowers during this pause;
an early riser, like you,
quietly watching the sun return.

Flamenco Workshop

An hour and a half of baile,
an hour and a half of palmas.

I come in late, squeezing my mother's Oldsmobile
into the parking lot by the barking dog.

Flamenco upstairs in the back.

Dark flame of a woman,
bright skirt, vamp scarf.
Her long-haired gypsy husband teaches the rhythms.

I put on my shoes,
brave in the back row in my jeans.
  She asks a little girl sitting on the side
    would she be dancing—You have a skirt on. You can dance.

A simple bulería for parties
 the steps, the arms,
  and the hips
only for the ladies—you men
just hold up your arms.

Any questions—next four.

¡Eso es!

Flamenco is ¡Yo soy!—I am.

I leave before the compás.

I have always been a dancer, but perhaps
I am not.
Or not any more.
It has been a hard year.

The shoes are in the closet,
in the corner with the tap shoes I bought
when the kids were still little.

I wonder about tango.
I hear it is a dance of loss.

Can Memory Sleep
    (refridgerator magnet poem)

why
you ask him

must naked time see
chance truth

and not give this body
that little night

do white bones
mean green longing

old man with a story
read me my page

never say soon

Cynthia McCain's poems have appeared in *Blue Heron Review,* *HEART,* *The Rumpus,* and *Halfway Down the Stairs,* among other publications. Her first chapbook, *Woman and Horse,* appeared in 2019.

Following a long career as a forest ecologist in the Pacific Northwest, she now lives in the country outside Corvallis, Oregon, where it's quiet, there are a lot of birds, and it's easy to go for walks.

www.ingramcontent.com/pod-product-compliance
Lightning Source LLC
LaVergne TN
LVHW041557070426
835507LV00011B/1151